Love to Win

from Alice

About the Book

The mother giraffe was about to give birth to her baby. She was hidden safely among the trees. Six females stood guard around her, ready to attack any predator that came near.

Unlike most baby animals, the giraffe's birth will include a five-and-a-half-foot fall to the ground, for the mother giraffe remains standing during its birth. Her baby, already six feet tall and 150 pounds, will soon be able to run across the African plains at a speed of 35 miles an hour. Someday he will grow to eighteen feet and weigh 2,000 pounds—a huge bull ready to lead a herd.

Alice L. Hopf and Patricia Collins have created a fascinating life cycle of an amazing and much-admired animal—the giraffe.

biography of a
Giraffe

by *Alice L. Hopf*
etchings by *Patricia Collins*

G.P. Putnam's Sons / New York

Published simultaneously
in Canada by Longman Canada, Limited, Toronto.
PRINTED IN THE UNITED STATES OF AMERICA
07211
Library of Congress Cataloging in Publication Data
Hopf, Alice Lightner, Biography of a giraffe
(Nature Biography)
SUMMARY: Follows the life cycle of a giraffe on the
African plain from his birth to the time he becomes the
undeniable leader of his own herd.
1.   Giraffes—Juvenile literature.   [1.   Giraffes]
I.   Collins, Patricia.   II.   Title.
QL737.U56H66   1978   599'.7357   76–52934
ISBN 0-399-61088-X lib. bdg.

This is for Karl Fredric, with love

The mother giraffe had found a safe hiding place. She was hidden among the trees that dotted the vast African plain on which she lived. Her long neck allowed her to look over the tops of the branches to see if an enemy was approaching. She knew she must stay hidden here until her baby was safely born. From nearby she heard the shrill laughter of a hyena. In the distance a lion roared.

As the giraffe stood quietly among the trees, another giraffe from the herd found her, and then another and another. Soon there were six female giraffes standing around her. They made a strong wall of legs and swinging necks. They would protect her from the attack of any predator.

The mother giraffe strained and heaved. The baby was being pushed out of the mother's hindquarters through the birth canal. Soon two little legs appeared from her rear. Another push and a head came with them. The little calf hung head downward until the mother gave one big, final heave. Then the whole baby slid out and fell—five and a half feet to the ground!

When the baby giraffe hit the ground, the blow started it breathing. The sudden jerk also broke the umbilical cord. The baby had been fastened to its mother by this cord. Now the mother giraffe turned around and spread her long front legs. She lowered her head and began to lick her baby all over to clean it.

After a while the baby giraffe tried to get to its feet. It tried several times, but each time it fell over. In about twenty-five minutes it was able to stand and walk about. It staggered around its mother while she licked it. It was a little male calf. Now the other giraffes came closer. They nuzzled the new calf and welcomed him into the herd. Within an hour, the baby had found his mother's teats and was having his first drink of milk. It was a long drink. It lasted almost ten minutes.

The baby giraffe was almost six feet tall at birth, and he weighed about 150 pounds. But he was tiny compared to the adult giraffes. Giraffes have five different spot patterns, and often there are several

patterns in the same herd. Some of the giraffes in this herd had large, dark brown spots, separated by thin white or yellow lines. But the new baby had little leaf-shaped spots all over his body. The spots were pale on the baby's woolly hair, but they would darken as he grew older.

For the first two days, the mother giraffe followed her baby about. She nudged him to go the way she wanted. But after two days he had learned to know her smell, so he could follow her. He ran after her and kept up with the browsing herd. When she called him with her peculiar whistle, he came.

At first the little calf got his legs mixed up when he ran. He had to learn how to

handle his long legs. At times he tripped and fell on his nose. But soon he found that he must move the two legs on one side and then the two on the other.

When he was three weeks old, he began to eat leaves. He watched the older calves browsing from the lower branches of a bush, and he tried to do the same. Soon he was eating this new food because he liked it, but he still went back to his mother for milk.

There were twelve giraffes in the herd, spread out over a wide area. Giraffes can stay farther apart than most herd animals because their long legs and necks allow them to see far across the plain. Their keen eyes, with the long lashes, can see a

long way and keep in touch with other members of the herd. In times of danger they can run thirty-five miles an hour and seem to float across the plain.

The little leaf-spotted giraffe soon learned to know all the members of his herd. He recognized the huge bull giraffe who was the leader. He had big horns on a big, heavy head. He swung his head threateningly at any predator that came near. He swung it at any giraffe that disputed his rule or got in his way.

But the big male did not chase his females around as many other herd animals do. The giraffe herd moved about over the plain in a free and easy group. Most of the females followed the big male. But now

and then one would wander away, perhaps to join another giraffe herd in another area. Sometimes a strange new giraffe would appear and join the herd. As long as it was not another bull come to dispute his leadership, the big male did not object.

The new little calf often watched the big bull giraffe. He was eighteen feet tall and weighed over 2,000 pounds. When he came near, the leaf-spotted baby got out of the way. Sometimes he hid between his mother's legs. This was his safest place. He could look out from underneath his mother and watch the big bull chase away the lurking hyenas. They knew that one blow from that heavy head could knock them flying. One kick could break their backs. They crept away to find easier prey.

Although the giraffes lived on the grassy plain, they did not eat grass. Their legs were too long for them to reach the ground. Instead, they ate the leaves of trees. All around them were little islands of trees. There were acacia trees and umbrella trees and sausage trees. The herd moved from one group of trees to another. They ate the topmost leaves and branches.

The calf's mother stood tall among the trees, daintily picking off leaves from the top. Two other giraffes were eating from the same tree. Only their heads could be seen. They looked like a family sitting around a dinner table as they picked off the best leaves from the very top. All the

time, their keen eyes watched the plain in all directions. It would be hard for a predator to approach unnoticed.

Acacia trees have many thorns and sharp spikes, but this did not bother the mother giraffe. Her seventeen-inch-long tongue reached out and pulled leaves and twigs into her mouth. Her strong, grasping lips broke them off so she could swallow them. She hardly noticed the thorns and spikes. She swallowed all her food quickly, without chewing. Giraffes are ruminants. They have four stomachs. When they are browsing, they eat quickly, not stopping to chew. Later, when they are resting in a safe place, they bring the food back into their mouths and chew it over again. Like the

cow, they chew their cud. When the leaves are well chewed the second time, they go down into the other stomachs to be digested.

When the sun rose higher and the day became hot, the giraffes moved to a more sheltered spot. There they stood quietly and chewed their cud. The mother giraffe groomed her calf. She licked and bit his coat to get rid of loose hair and bugs. She also groomed herself. Sometimes she straddled a thorny bush in order to scratch her stomach. Some of the herd slept for a few minutes at a time. They rested their heavy heads on the trees. But there was always one giraffe awake and watchful.

The little leaf-spotted calf did not care about resting. He nuzzled his mother. He drank milk from her teats. Then he wanted to play. There were two other calves in the herd. They were older and bigger, but they let the new calf play with them. They jumped and bucked. They chased each other around the resting herd. They investigated everything that moved. Sometimes they chased a lizard into its hole. Sometimes a little bat-eared fox caught their attention. Giraffes are very curious animals.

The calves spent a lot of time playing while their parents browsed. Often the big giraffes moved a good distance away. At such times, one of the older female

giraffes stayed with the young ones. She kept careful watch so that no harm would come to them. The mother giraffes watched from a distance. They always knew where to find their babies. They trusted the "nurse" giraffe to take care of the young calves.

Each day the giraffes went to a water-hole. They could go several days without water if necessary. If there was a drought and the foliage on the plain turned brown, all the animals would have to move to a greener place, no matter how far away. Then the giraffes could travel a long way between drinks. But now the water-hole was full, and they went there once a

day. They were careful to choose a time when other animals were not around. It would be very dangerous if an enemy should find them now. The giraffes had to kneel or spread their front legs very far apart in order to reach the water. In such positions a hunting lion would find them easy victims.

The mother giraffe never waded out into the water, for giraffes cannot swim and they are afraid of getting stuck in the mud. But one day, when the leaf-spotted giraffe was a bit older, he ventured into the water when he went for a drink. His mother wagged her ears and signaled to him with little movements. She even whistled softly, but he paid no attention. All at

once, he found that he could not pull his front legs out of the mud! He began to struggle, and bleated to his mother for help. But she only whistled more urgently for him to come back.

The little calf was very frightened. He had never been held down like this before. He had always been able to run and jump as he pleased. Now his two front legs were held by a mysterious force. He wriggled and pulled backward. Finally he gave a terrific jump backward and his two front feet popped out of the mud. He almost fell on his back. But he gave a quick, agile turn and landed on his feet near the shore. He had learned about water and mud. Never again would he wade out into a lake or river.

After they had been to the waterhole, the giraffes often went to a salt lick. The herd knew all the best places. The young calf watched as his mother filled her mouth with the saline earth, then raised her head to let the delicious flavor trickle down her throat. He put out his tongue and licked a salty rock. It tasted good. He licked some more. It was a special, pleasing taste.

At night, the giraffes came closer together. Now hearing and smell were more important in looking out for enemies. The giraffes seldom slept. Sometimes they took short naps, closing their eyes for a few minutes. Then they quickly came alert again. Only rarely did they lie down, for

they could easily be attacked in that position. When the mother giraffe lay down, she first knelt with her forelegs, then the rest of her body sank to the ground. She rested with her forelegs tucked up on one side or folded under her body. The calf slept beside her with his neck turned around so that his head rested on his back.

One night something alerted the herd. A menacing sound came to them. From quite near at hand they heard a low gurgle that rose into the shrill laugh of the hyena. It was answered from another direction. A pack of hyenas was out hunting! The giraffes began to move away. The leaf-spotted calf jumped up quickly. Only the

mother giraffe was lying down. She began to get to her feet, but it was difficult. First she pulled her long neck back as far as she could. Then she thrust it forward. This motion got her to her front knees. Again her neck jerked back and forth as she got her hind legs up. A final jerk got her onto her front feet.

But now the hyenas were closer. The young giraffe did not know what to do. He wanted to stay close to his mother, but he also wanted to run from the attacking beasts. Suddenly the big bull giraffe was with them. His huge body seemed to blot out the stars. He stood between the mother giraffe and the hyenas. He swung his long neck at them. He hit one attacker and sent it flying a dozen yards away. The

hyena landed in a bush and limped painfully off. As the big bull turned to follow the herd, he gave a mighty kick at a hyena that had come too close. The predator lay howling in the dust with a broken leg. The mother giraffe had escaped. She was running off into the night with her half-grown calf close behind her.

The giraffe herd wandered across the plain with many other animals. A family of brightly striped zebras grazed together nearby. There were ostriches and other large, walking birds. Even some wildebeests could be seen—big animals that looked like buffalo but were really a kind of antelope. They snorted and ran wildly when they were frightened. And there were smaller antelopes that jumped high in the air when they ran, making a graceful curve. These were impalas.

The leaf-spotted calf learned to know all these animals. He played with the young zebras and antelopes. He grew taller every day. His little horns, only knobs when he was born, began to grow bigger. At first they were loose and moved around under his skin, but soon they became anchored to his skull. Giraffe horns are different from those of other animals. They begin with soft cartilage. But as they grow, the cartilage becomes bone, starting at the tips and spreading downward. By the time the calf was four years old, his horns would be part of his skull. In a female, this might take

seven years. Giraffes also have a third horn in the middle, which is larger in the males.

As the herds of many kinds of animals grazed on the plain, brightly colored tick birds rode on their backs. Some had red beaks, and some yellow. They walked along the backs of the zebras and wildebeests, looking for ticks and other parasites. They got a meal while ridding the animals of these annoying insects. They climbed up and down the long necks of the giraffes. As the leaf-spotted calf grew older and bigger, the tick birds began to pay attention to him. He soon became used to having a bird clinging to his neck. He knew it was eating those biting insects. He also noticed that if danger threatened, the birds would

fly up, screeching loudly. They were friends of the giraffes. They helped the grazing animals.

Each year the leaf-spotted calf watched his father chase away other male giraffes. There was nothing hurried or vicious about it. When another bull appeared, the two would begin to show off. They stood a few yards apart, stiff-legged and with necks rigid. Each one tried to look bigger than the other. They leaned against each other, pushing with their shoulders.

As the young calf grew older, he began to spend more time with other young male giraffes. They moved about in a different group. They played at fighting, copying the things the big bull was doing. The

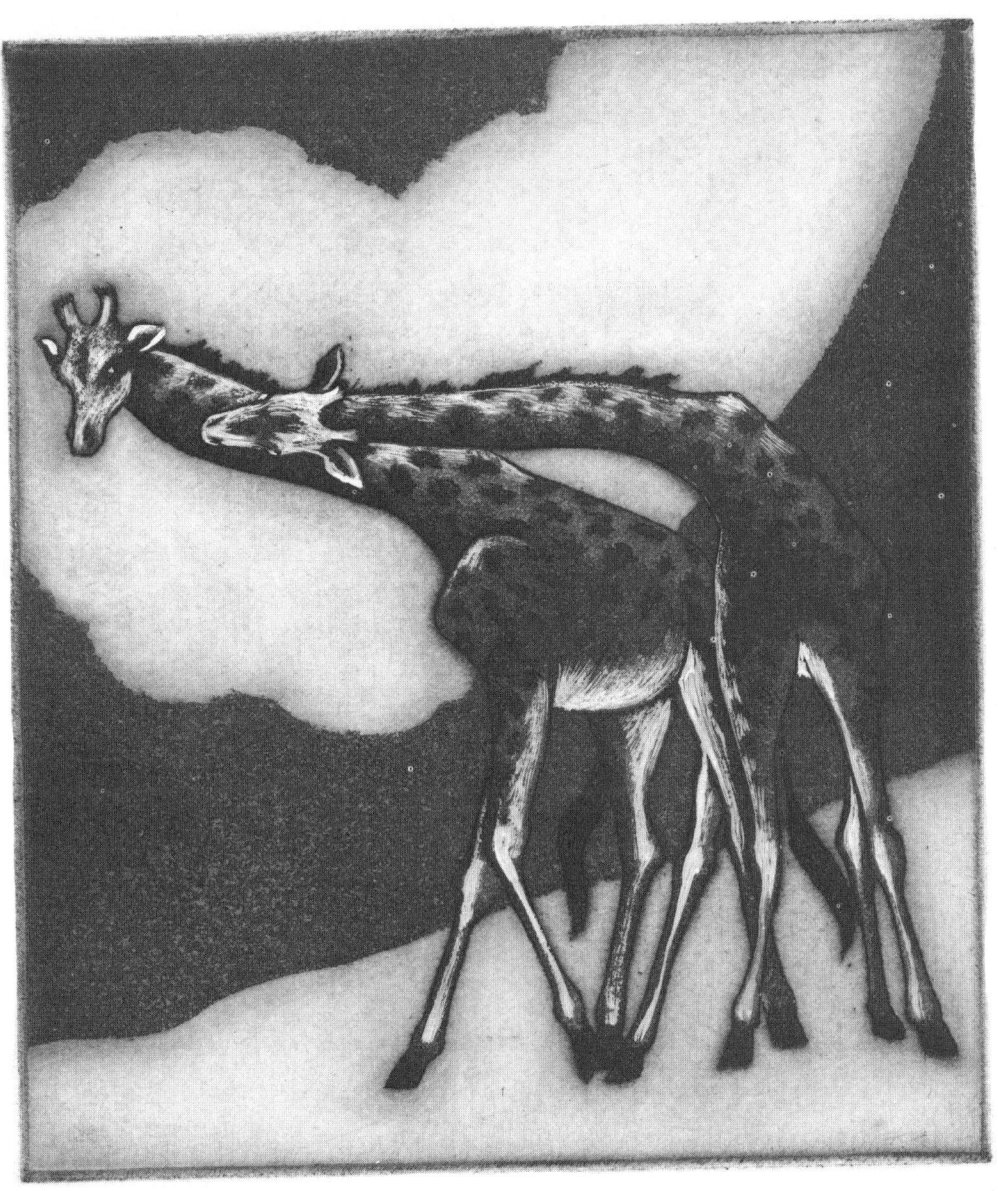

young giraffe was no longer a calf. He had become an adult. He was almost as big as his father, and he swung his head at the other young bulls in mock combat. He was especially friendly with the young bull that had grown up with him in his old herd. The two always browsed near each other. If they fought, it was only in play. Sometimes their necks became wound around each other. Then they would stop fighting and go back to eating.

One day the two young giraffes wandered away from the rest of their group. They wandered across the plain until they came to an area of farming and houses. They had never seen anything like this before. There were roads with scattered

houses along them. There were fields with grain and vegetables growing in them. The giraffes were curious about these things. They walked across the road from field to field.

To the giraffes it looked as if vines grew between the trees that bordered the road. The leaf-spotted giraffe knew all about trees and vines. He pushed through and found his neck blocked by a strange, tough vine that seemed to run between the trees. This wasn't like anything he had seen before. The other giraffe ducked his head to get under the strange vine, but the leaf-spotted giraffe was caught. He pushed and pushed.

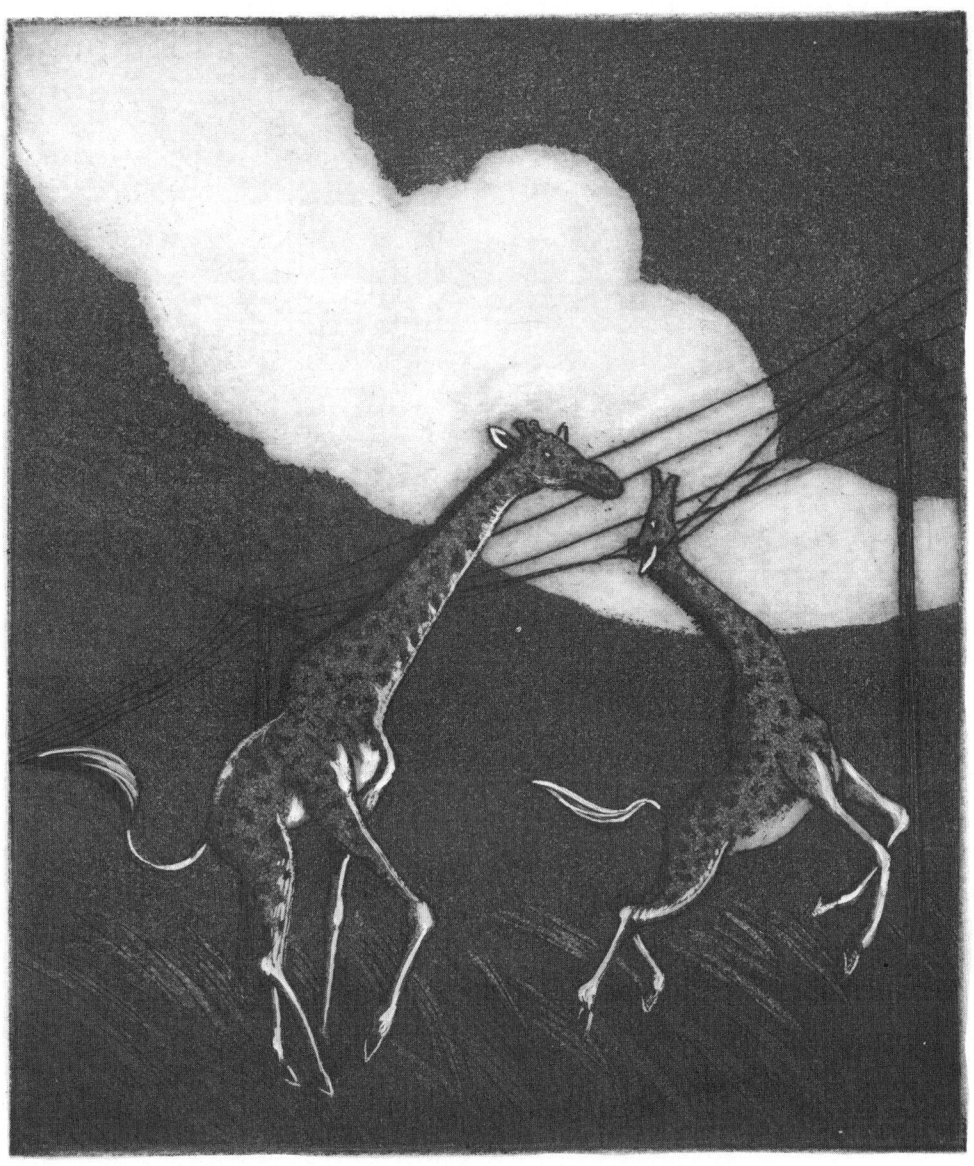

Tearing noises frightened him and he pushed harder. Giraffes are very strong. Soon he had pulled all the telephone wires down from their poles. He was angry at this strange vine that had caught him and would not let him pass. He trampled the ground. Then he backed up and escaped into the road.

Telephone service was broken down and two men were sent to find the cause and make repairs. When they arrived at the break, they saw what had happened. They were familiar with this situation. Two giraffes were standing in the road, chewing their cuds and looking around. The driver of the car moved slowly toward the animals, hoping to scare them away. But the leaf-spotted giraffe was still angry. He had

been almost strangled by the strange vine, and now here was a strange beast creeping up on him. When the car was almost upon him, the bull kicked. His hoof delivered a smashing blow. The hood of the car caved in. The motor conked out. Now the men had a car to repair, as well as the telephone line.

The two giraffes galloped away across the plain. They found their way back to the wild. After wandering for several days, they came upon a female giraffe with a young calf. She had left her herd and the two were wandering alone in dangerous country. The two bulls stayed with the cow and her calf. They formed a little herd. The bulls would help protect the young calf.

The leaf-spotted giraffe discovered that the cow had a lovely smell. He began to follow her about. When she stopped, he raised a foreleg and gently tapped her on her hindleg. When she ran off, he still followed. He lowered his head and rested it against her side. Sometimes he gave a low cough. If the other bull tried to follow, too, he shook his head at him threateningly. After several hours of chasing, the cow giraffe stood still when the leaf-spotted bull poked her with his foot. This was the signal that she was ready for mating, and the bull mounted her. Now he had his own cow. Now he had the beginning of his herd.

From time to time other female giraffes appeared and joined the leaf-spotted bull's herd. The other bull stayed around the edge and moved with the herd, but he did not dispute the leadership of the leaf-spotted bull.

But one day a new bull giraffe appeared—a stranger. He tried to take over the small herd and to chase the two bulls away. The leaf-spotted bull pushed up to him and the battle soon turned into a head-slamming contest. Each bull swung his head with great force, hitting the other bull's neck and body. Each jabbed his horns at his opponent's neck and shoulders. The leaf-spotted bull tried to dodge the painful head-slams, but that was not easy to do.

Still, he would not give up. This was his herd and he was going to keep it! Finally, he landed an especially hard blow on the other giraffe's body. The invader was knocked down. He lay unconscious in the dust for twenty minutes.

The leaf-spotted giraffe led his herd away. He knew that there would be no more trouble from that bull giraffe. He also knew he would be able to defend his herd from other thieving bulls or from any hungry predators that might turn up on the African plain.

About the Author

ALICE L. HOPF is equally at home writing science fiction (under her maiden name, A.M. Lightner) and writing about nature. She is a member of the Lepidopterists Society, the New York Entomological Society, and the Audubon Society. She has written several other nature and animal books for Putnam's, including *Biography of an American Reindeer* and *Biography of an Armadillo*.

About the Artist

PATRICIA COLLINS has illustrated numerous books of a scientific nature. Her etchings reflect her interest in how animals and plants adapt to their environment. Ms. Collins lives with her family in a converted cranberry factory in Duxbury, Massachusetts.